Meta Work

Anastasia Wasko

PLANET DUST
ENTERPRISES

Meta Work

Anastasia Wasko

© 2021 Anastasia Wasko

Published by Planet Dust Enterprises

ISBN 978-0-578-97179-7

Cover design & layout by Sharon Wasko Graphic Design

Acknowledgements

Thanks, mom and Frankenstein, for being two diametrically opposing influences. Your energies galvanized a breakthrough in my personhood.

Thanks, Sam Talbot, for being the "Eureka! You've got something here!" reader. Your enthusiasm and encouragement set this project in motion toward publication.

Thanks, Sharon Wasko (no relation that we can figure out), for the design and cover. Your enthusiasm and encouragement brought this project to public consumption.

Thank you, Jean-Paul Garnier and Zara Kand, for having me in your home. It was a week steeped in creative essence that held the memoir as it turned from memoir to autofiction.

Thank you, New York City, for having me home over the winter of 2020/2021 to finish this work.

Om lokah samastah sukinoh bhavantu //
May all beings everywhere be happy and free

Introduction:
Autofiction for transformation

Autofiction is the container I needed for the transformation I sought. Memoir could not give it to me. Memoir is too established; I needed something that offered less form. Autofiction is autobiographical fiction; the work starts with truth, ends in truth, weaves in untruth, and leaves the writer with catharsis, the resonance of which the few people who appreciate autofiction will imbibe.

I started this manuscript ten years ago in a launch toward verisimilitude—I wanted to create a collection of words that mirrored the way that I experienced reality. I needed a reflection of the chaos of my inner world; I hoped to find a truth to articulate in it. I began in memoir because that was the form offered to me then. Other writers had said they found their truth by writing memoir; readers had said they learned about their truth from reading memoir. But over the course of this work, I received little validation as writer or from readers. Ten years of a creative writing and reading practice in memoir, left me feeling limited by narrative form. Memoir couldn't hold my vision of my world.

I switched the label of the form; I briefly named this manuscript a work of speculative memoir to allow for the fantastic elements. It was then I realized what I was doing wasn't writing to find truth in chaos. The truth is the chaos itself. I abandoned the manuscript as a memoir completely. I turned the manuscript into autofiction as an act of wholeness. This allowed me to write as I desired so that I might create the verisimilitude I intended. Here, the goal of creative expression was met: create a piece of writing to show that chaos was rooted in truth, questioned truth, weaved in untruth, and through integrating all these parts, I achieved catharsis. This is meta-work.

I ended the writing of this manuscript when I felt the desired catharsis. The only way out of chaos is through it—and this piece of autofiction is an offering of what it's like to experience that process. A sublimation of the mirror, if you will. *Meta Work* enters creative expression (here, through writing) as an integral part of the transformation process that leads to healing. The creative expression process happened with support from professional sources, too: mental health care, holistic health care, and allopathic health care. The act of creative expression is like turning a pressure valve to release. The intrapsychic forces have a strong effect on the mind and body; when those forces are not attended to, they accumulate into maladaptive structures and cause dis-ease.

The point at which I decided I was ready to put this manuscript out in the world is the point at which the work took on a life of its own. I realized this autofiction is a gateway. I offer, through this translation of direct experience to page, a chance to cultivate empathy. I am here on these pages, but I am not alone. I am one of many who have had challenging experiences with mental health. We need more empathy to support each other's journey to wholeness. I'm on this trip for the long haul. I bring bipolar disorder, invite you to live with it, as it takes up residence in my mind. I bring trauma, conveyed as a constellation of points in time that float upon waves of emotional and cognitive dissonance. I bring the consideration that the disorder and trauma (collectively, the chaos) is not me; there is a "me" inside of the chaos. I gift you with the key to unlocking the gateway to understanding this. I hope you see yourself in here, too.

13: New York City

Fat Canada geese ran through the Great Meadow in Central Park. A small, black deli plastic bag floated up over an American elm tree. The summer heat hung in the thick City air. Young kids played in the fountain with a graffitied Corinthian-style column spout. The tags were an unreadable mess of words scribbled in black and red ink. A teenage girl wearing ballet flats and too-tight jeans walked by; she casually dropped a sandwich wrapper. The paper fell as she stuffed a last crust of bread into her mouth as she looked at her phone. A mother spread a blanket over a patch of worn grass and then laid her baby on it. The baby had a hat and booties and onesie on. She reached for the dirt and the mother smacked her hand.

A middle-aged man sat down next to me on the bench. He placed his leather satchel between his hip and the black iron rail.

I turned to him and said: "In the beginning and in the end, there is sound. My body has a sound. The notes came from my parents. They crash boom banged and now I have an audio imprint on the universe. It is a track that I hear and don't hear. How cool is that?"

The man, who wore thick-rimmed, clear-acrylic-framed glasses and a put-together dark maroon pantsuit that showed his naked ankles and shiny lace-free leather shoes, looked down his nose at me: "I have no idea what you just said." Then he picked up his satchel and left.

"New York City is pulling the strings to the world inside me," I said as he walked away.

I turned my head and pressed the ballpoint pen hard and pulled it across the blank page so the blue ink streaked. I waited for the words to come out and play. A pigeon's shit bomb plopped on top of my head. The black plastic deli bag reached over the elm tree as it rode the wind of the breezy summer afternoon. My pen pressed to paper. I was thirteen years old, impervious to the world outside.

28: New York City

The computer screen was in front of me, full—documents with dancing words and blinking cursors, work unfinished; an Internet browser with several open tabs, thought trains derailed; e-mail pop outs, half-written messages. I felt a sour coffee smell trying to crawl up my nose, and my ears rang numb from the murmur of fluorescent lighting pushing a low-pitch whine into my brain.

I leaned back in the wide-seat office chair, and I tried to roll a nausea knot out of my chest. I burped.

I was there to work—today a storyboard for a commercial and a one-page journal ad. It was the umpteenth time this agency had brought me in to do what other freelancers do: produce tangible things in the electronic form: assemble pixels on a page: infuse the pixel bits with so-called meaningful information: craft said meaningful information to a determined function while abiding trendy what's-cool-now advertising agency culture, the client disconsolate and-uncontestable demands, the account execs who bear news of said disconsolate-and-uncontestable demands by calling urgent, impromptu "team meetings" at precisely 6pm, minutes before everyone left for the day.

Work made me feel important. I produced tangible things in the electronic form: assembled pixels on a page: infused the pixel bits with so-called meaningful information: crafted said meaningful information to a determined function. The advertising agency work paid my bills. That was my occupation. I wrote, too. Writing was my life work. I took my job to explore my inner world very seriously.

The nausea intensified in my chest.

My inner world took me very seriously, too. I have a relationship with it, and this nausea is the incontestable demand that it puts on me. It needed a meeting. It wanted out.

I tried to ground, shift out of my head and body, reorient myself by mapping time and space: I noted that I didn't feel comfortable in the temporary workspace—I usually didn't bother to settle into comfort. I was a gig-based professional, so I always landed a cubicle. This cubicle had walls made of canvas and foam. I nimbly pushed a push pin on the cubicle wall just to make the sound, which was like popcorn popping—pop!

The freelance editor who occupied this space before me had left bits and pieces behind. Droppings, I called them. I made a visual inventory: orphan pen, left behind the dusty keyboard; itinerant herbal tea bags that caused me to question the drinking habits of the previous editor—coffee, editors need coffee—and notes: large, full sheets of paper and small, Post-it Notes stuck to the cubicle wall. Style tips (bold the headline on each page!) and brand nuances (make sure the medication is spelled correctly! client hates it when we misspell the product name—circled twice). I took another push pin out of the small plastic box on the desk; I jabbed quickly at a particularly hard-to-read piece of chicken scratch that was hanging: POP.

Something broke inside of me; the nausea roared. I looked around. There was a line of sight from an opening in my cubicle to the atrium of the building. Walls of glass—all seven floors—gave me an ability to see to other levels of cubicles. So many floors of humans working. I'm watching from the other side of the glass.

I know how to anticipate the mental explosions. I feel them creeping in. When they threaten to eclipse my connection to the *working* world. I need to get gone.

I quickly threw up my hands, held them out, steadied myself. I inhaled, and along with some breath came a few wisps of the smell of a temporary-team member-colleague's Indian food lunch with ghost coffee that haunted the ventilation system.

My eyes felt dull. What time was it anyway? Hours ago, I'd given up looking at the numbers—the clock—because 2pm could be 2am and I wouldn't know the difference. Artificial light, closed space, cubicle farm: work.

I need to get outside.

I could hear the transient-to-me colleague over the faux wall laughing at something. She called to me, said she found something funny online, but I ignored her. I couldn't be bothered. Then she came around to my side of the cubicle, stood me up, and literally dragged me back to her computer. She made me watch the video that caused her joy. I feigned laughter. She, transient-to-me colleague, my boss, didn't stop talking the whole time, over the video, over the hum of fluorescent lights, the blah blah blah consistent, blah blah blah.

And then the sounds out of her mouth changed: "The

document"—the word jerked me into a necessary conversation.

"Yes," I replied, "what about it?"

"Have you finished editing yet? Have you cross-checked the style guide? The clinical data for the medication?"

"Right," I replied. "I just need a little more time."

"Finish it for the team meeting at the end of the day."

—I already knew that—

"I want to review it before the meeting"

—I knew the colleague would say that, too—

"And make sure it's done."

I assured her it would be, that she would have time to review it, and then excused myself. "I need to step out for a moment."

I went back to my desk, pulled my witty graphic t-shirt down, adjusted the folds around my belly, wrapped my black sweater around me tightly and fastened it with a white belt. I draped earbuds around my neck—clipped the mp3 player to my sweater, no music yet—and wrapped a scarf over my shoulders. I grabbed my neon-rainbow-zebra-striped pan-am style bag and took the building pass out, clipped that to the waist of my skirt, which had bunched up on the tops of my black knee-high cowboy boots. I kicked my legs one at a time and the skirt resettled.

"Be right back!" I said quickly to the transient-to-me colleague over the clinical cubicle wall. I moved too fast to allow her the chance to respond.

Fast: through the measured rows of squares—fast, fast, fast, stifling my gag reflex—fast, so all that I saw in the office was a blur of white, gray, and beige.

I reached the elevator bank—six individual carriages—a set of doors opened in the one nearest me: I got in and was alone.

I pressed the down button, the close-door button, the down button again. A feeling of descent pressed my body with the mechanical ride. Seven floors. The nausea knot in my chest buoyed up to my throat, and when the elevator doors opened at the black-marbled lobby, the knot released. I got out, crossed the marble lobby, passed the security desk, went through brass revolving doors, and walked out onto the New York City street. I opened my mouth, stuck out my tongue, and stretched it out hard.

I started to breathe again as City noises melted into my skin: dripped from the sky, echoed off the streets, rappelled on the buildings. Around me, passersby, moving bits of women with fake hair and men with waxed eyebrows and sub-burby moms with daughters on their first City shopping trip.

I turned right, started to walk down the block, headed eastward into the thick of Herald Square. I turned again at the corner, left, crossed the intersection, continued.

Overflowing garbage bins, empty telephone consoles; unmarked doors crammed together with signs full of letters that look like symbols to me; bright colors; the smell of fish; the sounds of a language that I cannot understand.

I tapped the mp3 player hooked to my sweater. I reached into my scarf, fished out the ear buds, and stuck them in my ear. *Play.* Pressed up the volume.

Goopy electronica became louder; a metallic peeping sound: consumed into the City experience. Faster: the periphery dissolves: the sounds in space: limbo-like: nothing but the grey around me: in that grey, things alive. The City, big breathing rock, cavernous; streets and sidewalks—rivers.

On the sidewalks, gum spots: holes that hide things inside… aquatic monsters. Crocodiles. They swam directly beneath my feet.

I

walked

on.

Fuck. What time was it?

How long was I gone from the gig? Work? I had been walking down a street in Little Korea with my nose turned up to the sky and a giant smile on my face for a while. My oversized glasses concealed my squinty eyes.

I can't just walk off a job, right? Is that even a question I can ask? I grew up in working class culture. If someone just walked off a job, there was something *wrong* with them.

I remembered that work I had to do before the end of the day. *Fuck.* I had to go: I quickly retraced my steps: half memory, half looking at the buildings to orientate myself.

I took a deep breath before I walked through the revolving doors, back into the black-marbled lobby—sunlight left behind for artificial light. Live air became recycled air. Open space became a box: I pressed the button for the elevator. Rectangular doors opened, into the rectangular carriage, I stepped. Doors closed. I pressed up. The nausea returned.

Later that day—

"The client decided they're going in another direction. We're going to let you go," my transient colleague, boss of the week said. She leaned on the popcorn-cubicle wall. It crunched. "We'll call you back when we need more help."

"Okay, no problem," I said, nonchalantly.

And just like that, my gig got a red light—it stopped—and I was let go. I happily gathered my droppings from the cubicle, threw a few extra pens and Post-its in my zebra bag, waved, gave well-wishes to the temporary colleagues, assured them I would be back. I left the office thinking "Phew!"

Just like I always did. My head was fuzzy, wondering where my next gig would be, wondering whom to call and tell I was available... because fuck, rent was due soon and now I was going to be short. But I was preoccupied—just like I always was in the City.

I walked down Seventh Ave, paused at the north-east corner of Thirty-third, and then, with one small surge, approached the great steps of Madison Square Garden: the behemoth entertainment venue and transportation hub squeezed onto one City block.

It was rush hour.

Cacophony of honk! shove! yell! swish! zoom! beep! whistle! Rattle and hum. Rattle and hum.

My mind exploded in response: vectors crashing and exploding and sending expletive bangs! Buildings churning human forms out, humanized geometric forms slithering along the sidewalks of pavement-river-streets, creeping back, commuting back to their homes...

A slight pulse, through the soles of my feet, told me another monster was waking below, waking inside me: I looked down, and I (in my mind) saw a snake in the belly of the stone, heard the snake below me... a muted rumble, a hisssss, a subway car slithering through the tunnel innards of the City.

I watched my hands take a white plastic Duane Reade bag from my canvas tote, rip the plastic in half, lay it on the ground, my physical body lets itself down, it settles on the belly, butt up, legs hanging over the edge of the steps, toes touching a step.

My eyes closed. I imagined the cold platform, a warm patch of moss, that I'm basking in warmth, that I'm surrounded by bright green grass, a golden yellow sun, and pink and blue flowers, and below me, a very large snake guards me in this Madison Square Garden.

The sound of scuffling up the steps becomes the sound of wings flapping. Butterflies in the wind... soft breezes of air laps against my pant legs, I drift into the sounds of the City that Never Sleeps, the City of Artificial Light and Windows that Are Mirrors into Other Versions of Ourselves—

A chill started to grow through my skin.

The dark sky had completely descended and the electric glow of billboards didn't stave off the darkness in me. I had become sufficiently something, my physical body achy, shook to the bones it felt like. I had to get out of the cold. I couldn't grasp onto a thought—it happened like that sometimes—but my body hurt, and it needed warmth. I turned, and eyed the Borders book store up the steps. I could get warm in there. I went in.

"Borders is closing..." I hear suddenly, and I look at my watch, and three hours have passed.

Fuck.

I start to shuffle out with the others. This part is the hardest part of my day. I have to get on the train and go home.

It's only an avenue-block to Herald Square where I could catch my train back to Jersey City, where my apartment was.

I started out with a walk, then a canter, then a run—

But I was overcome.

The next thing I know I am standing at the door to my apartment. I look down and thank my feet; they remembered that this is where I needed to end up.

I went down the three small stairs and entered my basement apartment; I didn't turn on the lights as I fell face-down into my bed. Jacket on, sweater on, scarves on, laying on top of the blanket on the mattress, I slid my hand under my clothes unhooked my bra, and fell asleep with my cowboy boots on.

33: Kingston, NY

Sitting in the fourteen-seat, silver and maroon Suburban with a snow plow hook year-round: I was buckled in, and I had my hands under the lip of the bench seat. No, I didn't just have my hands under the bench seat—my fingers pressed into the polyester or vinyl or polyester-vinyl or whatever the material was. My fingers needed to grab on to something.

"Dad?" I said, half asking, half saying, fully calm.

"What?"

I couldn't see his head reaction—the damned headrest blocked a clear view.

"Dad, I want to talk to you about something." He didn't answer right away.

He drove. We wound down residential streets in the small town toward his construction business shop. There was nothing to see out of the window; I had seen it all before. Nothing changed, day in, day out. Dump trucks passed to the left and right.

Then he answered—

"What?"

There was a slight twitch to his head, which meant he might be in a jovial mood. Might. A staid head meant you might hit brick walls.

"I want to publish a book."

"You need a college degree."

"No, dad. You don't need a college degree. I have a plan figured out. I'm going to self-publish. That means I make it, not someone else. It's a new thing."

"I know a guy who makes books. He owes me a favor."

He was referring to the book binding shop, run by a Hungarian-American family, off the county highway.

"No, this is something different. The guy you know fixes old books. I want to do it on my own. I want to write a book. And then I want to publish it."

"You need a college degree."

"You don't have one. And you have your own company."

"You won't make money. Writing isn't work."

"Dad, I don't care. This is what I want to do."

Silence.

"But you want money now to do it."

"Pretty much."

"What figure are we talking about?"

"Well, I need to write it, and for that I need to live. And the production costs, you know. I'll self-publish and then I want to start a business writing. And I need a book to be my first thing to sell."

"But you don't know what you want to write about."

"That's not how it works. Writing isn't hour for hour work like you do. Give me time. Give me money. I will figure out how to write books and then I will write them. And then I will go to the City. The publishing industry is in the City."

"City people aren't our people."

"Dad, writing is a business. Lots of City people do it. I want to be in on that."

"Business runs on numbers," he said.

"Will you help me?"

"No."

I turned my head again, looked out the window. The small houses had lawns that were spotted with plastic ornaments and flower pots with overflowing geraniums and impatiens. Small cars, mostly Fords and Chevys, sat in driveways, next to Ford and Chevy pick-up trucks, next to wheelbarrows and woodpiles. Houses of families where patriarchs were construction workers, plumbers, electricians and matriarchs were housewives, bartenders, administrative assistants.

There was nothing to see out of the window; I had seen it all before. Nothing changed, day in, day out.

We rode the rest of the way in silence. We arrived at his shop, and I stayed in the Suburban, fuming and holding the edge of the bench seat.

"What next?" I muttered, watching him walk into the shop through the opened, oversized garage doors. He came back out with a Coors in hand, took a sip, and then started walking to the compound lot where machines were kept, stopping to talk with each employee. My uncle. The Colombian guy who's been working for my dad since I can remember. My older brother. They all wore dirty jeans, dirty work boots, and shirts with my last name on them.

I looked at the leather case on his front seat. It was a dinosaur—a car phone that plugged into the cigarette tray. I picked up the receiver, and the pile of yellow notebooks plus construction plans fell all over. Too much shit in the front seat. I fumed. I was young—Did I know what I would write about? No. I thought that telling him I wanted to write a book was better than telling him I wanted to write. I thought that a book would be something he could touch. Dad only worked with things he could see, could touch.

"Bah!" I pulled the receiver toward me and gently tugged on the cord to undo a kink. Calls from this phone were very expensive. I dialed my mom.

"He won't do it, mom," I said.

She picked right up on my thought: "It's asking a lot. You know that. Do you think we come from money?"

"I know, I know. We don't. But I need this." I put a subtle urge behind "need"—one tone, one small inflection, that only she would understand. "I can't stand to do anything else. I just need to be left alone with my thoughts. I will make a business out of them."

It's hard to judge facial expressions in conversations like this. The packets of data traveling from one cell phone to another don't seem to understand our needs for subtle clues. Damned machines. Then I heard a sigh.

"Fine. I'll call him tonight."

"Okay. Thanks."

We hung up. I dialed my mom again, asked her not to hang up for a while. She said "okay." I left the car phone on while I sat.

"That was a long time ago," I said, referring to the scene I was practicing for the reading later that night. My mom nodded. "I know advertising isn't the same as publishing, but at least I get to work with words every day. And I can write in between gigs. Like now." I sighed and put down the papers I was reading off of.

I wore a skimpy, lacy dress, a flashy number I had picked out for my reading. The house was cold and goosebumps dotted my arms. Mom kept curling my hair. The heat of the iron was nice because I felt her cold hands near my scalp—

"One Mississippi, two Mississippi," I counted. She laughed. It's an old game, I can remember as far back as five years old, Mom curling my hair, telling me to count Mississippis to time the curl. My nails were painted with an extra special OPI shade: chunky glitter—all for the performance.

"Do you think he would come to my reading?" I asked.

A shadow descended; I knew her face had turned. I didn't need to see it to feel it.

She didn't need to answer because I knew. My dad wasn't the type to come to readings, let alone pick up a book. He stayed as far away from things he didn't understand, and my creativity was no different. He was a builder and he, as a rule, didn't try to understand anything that was different than his every day. I used to tell him that reading was a way to get to know yourself. I asked him if he ever thought about that. He used to say that was all bullshit.

I gently reached up, touched the world ball-charm that hung on my necklace, shook it. A sound came out. Every time I heard the sound, I thought it was magic. The world itself was magic.

"You promise you're coming?" I asked my mom.

"Just text me shortly before you go on," she replied.

"Okay," I said. But I didn't expect her to show up. I had to ask; it was part of my routine.

Later that night, when I went on stage, I was still calm. My feet felt the ground through my cowboy boots. The curls on my head made me feel 6 feet tall. I squinted, but I didn't see my mom at the back.

I started to read, and then quickly looked up. It was for the effect. I knew the first lines, I've said them so many times. I saw black busts, sometimes faces, mostly it's blurry. I'm reading a story about my dad and the country dance hall that was inside of his shop, boot-scooting boogies next to Kubotas and excavator machines.

"North Jersey's largest raised dance floor," shouted the advertisement. "Straight off Route 80. My first lesson in marketing came from the dancehall. I used to enter the mailing list names on the word processor, print out the labels, stick 'em on mailers. I used to clean up, too. Vacuum, pick up plastic cups. There was a cheap plastic tablecloth that covered the refreshment table; it always took some elbow grease to get that thing sticky-less."

The audience laughed.

"The scuff marks on the dance floor followed a line. When I went the following morning, to clean, I imagined the ghosts of the dancers still there, the scuffs marking their spots in time and that the boot-scoot-and-stomped out dancers already danced." The audience laughed.

I finished the story with a description of me, a wide-eyed, fifteen-year-old girl who, with pockets stuffed with cash after cleaning, hopped the train and went to New York City to write.

The memory of the reading fresh on my mind—I wished I could stay on the stage, forever. But I had to work, and the City had jobs the small town didn't. I had become a long-distance commuter since I no longer lived there full time. I took short trips down for my short-term work gigs as a freelance editor at advertising agencies. Sometimes I stayed at an Airbnb if I booked a few consecutive days of work. It was a professional's way of life.

I felt a slowing down of the car, and I readied my suitcase and feet, just like I had readied my feet as I stood on the reading stage.

The train rolled into the station. The vibration beneath me changed.

I got up and exited the subway car, paused on the platform. The wheels of my small black hardtop rolled with a sticky sound. I pushed on the pull-up handle and grabbed the small side. I whisked my suit-case and me up the stairs in a practiced motion that felt natural and easy. Up, up, fast up the subway stairs because the station smelled like piss. As soon as I breached street level, a damp coolness of a spring City night hit my face. It felt good.

Which way to go?

I looked around. There was something about these storefronts, the slabs of stone, the shadows cast on the dirty sidewalks.

No, wait. Something about this was recognizable. Something...I double checked the address for my Airbnb. It said "Williamsburg neighborhood."

But instead of quiet in my ears, I started to hear a faint hissing, sort of like steam when it's coming out of radiators.

I slowed my walk, dragged my overnighter suitcase to a stop, paused on the street.

Gates to my left and right. Stoops cluttered with garbage, house-plants, Easter decorations: eggs, rabbits, eggs, rabbits. Happy Easter.

Then—a strong surge of nausea came over me. I recognized this place.

I took the print-out of my reservation from my pocket. I tripled checked that the description said the apartment was located in Williamsburg. But I put the address of the rental into my phone's GPS. It said I was in Greenpoint.

This was the one place in New York City I swore I would never come back to. A cold sweat overcame my body. I hated this neighborhood. I hated Greenpoint. I had crossed my heart and hoped to die to never return to this place… it held too many memories. I felt like I had been cheated. I cursed the booking and the misappropriated description on the website.

Okay, I thought. I need to do this. I need to sleep because I need to work tomorrow. I wondered if I could cancel the reservation: but it was nearly 9.00pm at night. And I was dead tired.

I started to wheel my suitcase again. I wasn't far from my destination.

When I arrived, I rang the buzzer, was let in to a newish building— one that had trendy modern windows and smooth concrete walls, unlike the crumbling brick brownstones that surrounded it—and I went up the stairs to the apartment. The girl who answered the door, aka the one who really lived there and was renting me her couch, was friendly, quiet, muted. I felt my brain go into a freeze, a sort of static white noise underneath; the girl started speaking to me, telling me about the shower, the kitchen, the area. It was tiny, mod, and well curated with orange and green vintage housewares and a dark wood table.

"—thanks," I cut in. "But I'm really only here to sleep."

She looked at me with eyes that I couldn't tell were tired, or dull, or both, or none. She pulled the belt of her kimono style bathrobe a little bit tighter, swung her blonde-with-black-roots hair back. "OK. Well goodnight," she said, turning, entering her own room, closing the door.

Paaaaaaaah, I exhaled. I looked at the futon, set under a large window. It was dark, I could see lights, but not whatever lay on the other side of the glass. I set my backpack down, my rolling suitcase next to it. I fetched my sleeping gear, went into the bathroom, changed, and brushed my teeth. I walked back to the living room, where the futon was, where the cell-like interior of this small City apartment was home for the night.

Time: 9.17pm. I just need to make it to sunrise.

I laid down and found the futon mattress flat. Uncomfortable. Hard against me, a person whose body tensed in a knot. I took my jacket, bunched it up, and stuck it under the pillow, but I still felt cramped and squashed and stretched. I became aware of a vibration that coursed through my body, from my fingers to my toes to the top of my head. I felt it coming. So I just lay there.

Somehow, I drifted off but I didn't dream. I woke up the next morning and I was instantly relieved: I had survived the night. Then I sprung up, quickly: I looked out the window. On the other side of the glass, the busy highway that bisected Brooklyn.

For fuck's sake, I thought. 278. The BQE, source of the buzzing last night. The vibrations coming from the round-the-clock busy high-way that straddled my old neighborhood.

I shuddered.

Suddenly I heard a creak. I glanced quickly over my shoulder, and saw my host. Her puffy eyes weren't quite open: "Morning," she mumbled.

"I'll be gone soon," I replied. I rushed myself to wake. I went into the bathroom, this time with my backpack, and shake-shimmied out of bed clothes and into day clothes. I dabbed on deodorant, brushed my teeth, splashed my face with water.

I was out of the apartment in less than fifteen minutes. In the light of day, I could see all the new developments, the behemoths of stone and glass and lights next to the small concrete stoops and lines of garbage pails. It was 7.30 in the morning. I couldn't go to the agency's office yet—I wasn't scheduled till 5pm. I had heard about a morning dance party, so I decided to go check that out. I could, at the least, sit in the corner and pass some time. The City's rhythms so early in the morning were people returning from clubs, or going to work, and I was somewhere between a nightmare and a day dream and it was too cold to sit outside and brood. So I got on the train.

10: Mount Hope, New Jersey

Dad drove his truck down the gravel driveway.

"Why can't I go back to mom's house?"

No answer.

"I want to go back to mom's house."

One of my brothers opened the door to the pick-up, and I got out, huffing and puffing.

"Do something useful, will ya?" he said over his shoulder, through the window of the red Ford pick-up truck as he pulled away. He was going back to his shop, his construction business. My two brothers sat next to him on the faded bench seat. The lot of them drove away—my dad told them he had work for them to do at the shop. I cried and complained the whole ride from my mom's house to dad's house. He dropped me off because he didn't want to deal with me. "The brat always gets her way," one of my brothers said, words trailing out the open window of the passenger side.

Same as it ever was.

The house was a dull grey modular, with a deck. Behind the deck, a small garden, pen for goats, pen for chickens. There was a massive trampoline on the side of the house. A few small machines were parked in the lot behind the house; everywhere, there were woods. The neighbor who lived across the street—an old man we called Mr. Cupchock—was a sort of hobo. He didn't have electric in his house. He had a dog—Pal—who rode shotgun in Mr. Cupchock's ancient blue minivan. There were a few trees that separated my dad's house from Mr. Cupchock's—better so, because the old man had so much stuff. Everywhere. Spilling out of his house. *What is it with old men and machine parts?*

I went inside the empty grey modular house to my bedroom, full of second-hand furniture. There was a long dresser with a tall mirror and a full-size bed that squeaked every time I sat in it. I hated the furniture because it wasn't mine—or, I didn't have a choice of the furniture in my room. I showed up one day and it was there. I had told my dad I didn't like it, and he replied that's all you get.

I decided to go for a walk on the trail. I took some books and my journal from my heavier bag full of clothes for a few nights stay, which I had packed when I was leaving my mom's house, and put them into a tote. I went into the kitchen and took a handful of granola bars from the pantry. I was planning to be gone for a while.

Ten minutes later, I was in an open space at the top of the path, a windy dirt trail that led up a steepish rocky slope. The tract of land was under high tension lines, so that's why we called it the high-tension line trail. From here, I could see the City, forty-five miles due east. It never moved. Some days I saw it, some days I didn't. I imagined the City from afar, not very much like the solitude of the woods, the quietness of the trails. I liked my perch up high, my view of the

City from a distance. It was as if it was there to watch over me. (At least that's what I thought.)

I opened my bag and took out a journal. My eyes started to blur with more tears, tears I couldn't control. Snot and drops landed on the journal pages. Although my mind was full, I couldn't bring myself to write. So I stood on top of a smooth grey rock—one I returned to every time I went to this place on the trail—and screamed so hard my throat hurt.

26: Northern New Jersey

The highway was a straight, grey line, expensive gas, darting cars. Billboard signs for Amish country, country fudge, and fishing charters. In sum, this and that. An hour on the road, and I was in a different world.

I leaned back, propped on an elbow, propped my right foot over the dashboard fan. I looked down at my bare foot, steady on the gas pedal. It's easier to drive in bare feet. I had rented a car, since I was not booked for a gig, and headed out of the City to get some distance from that which I loved and I hated. The concrete jungle was my bedfellow. It was the demon lover I couldn't shake, the one that ravaged me and left me bare. It was no way to live, but I didn't know any other way.

I was on the move in northern New Jersey.

The electronica—a smooth Chemical Brother's song, "Exit Planet Dust"—transformed the asphalt roadway to a pathway through space, and the car flew fast, and I had the volume turned way up, and I couldn't feel anything around me, and I was consumed by sound, and when I turned the music down, my ears shook, withdrawing, wanting more of the beats, but it was 4.45pm, and I had just arrived at a cheap motel, where I wanted to have a quiet place to pass the night.

I was checked out when I checked in; I don't even remember the attendant's face, the one who gave me keys and told me my room number. But there I was, suddenly aware, standing in a room that smelled a little like dust and mold and plastic. Why did these places always have a faux velour blanket in the tightly tucked bed dress? Why did I think that a headboard made out of pressed wood attached to the wall was creepy? The lamps matched. And the curtains look like they are cut from the same fabric as the blanket. Room cards, fixed television channels, pizza menu hanging below the inner keyhole.

I turned my heavy head. 9pm. Where did the time go? I had fallen asleep, lying on the mattress with the fries I had gotten earlier. My stomach grumbled. I heard the zoom zooooom of the cars outside… it takes me places… I'm tired, so I'm letting myself go to sleep, and on my way to sleep, I am starting to go into dreams… the pictures hung before my eyes. Pictures flashing in my eyes, hanging there, the memory camera taking pictures of me. And I am haunted. This is what I was trying to avoid. I wanted to run from myself, but I found me, the worst versions of me.

I jerk up, fully awake in the motel room bed.

I switch on the light, quickly dig out my journal and pencil—always a pencil—from my backpack, and I start to free write:

—dropped the pencil, scared.

I grabbed my head and gritted my teeth. The light in the room drifted to a shadow. My stomach rumbled again. The fries turned in my belly.

A bug splattered against a window. I heard a futile bzz, bzz. He hit the window—splat!—and fell into the pane on the exterior.

I woke up without the alarm, got up quickly, re-gathered my stuff quickly. I must have slept stiff as a board because the blankets— which I had laid down over the motel's sheets—were still in their perfect fold. Long rectangles, like mats. I threw my pillow on top, rolled them together, made a quick knot with a piece of ribbon. I cleared the bathroom twice—for fear of forgetting the Guccis, my trademark oversized sunglasses—and I quickly dropped everything off in the rental car, directly outside.

"Won't even bother with the free continental," I say to myself, out loud, while envisioning trays of plastic-like croissants, pastries, and fruit sitting on a table in the check-in lounge.

I leave the key in the room and the door shuts.

9am.

I drove for a few miles. I knew exactly where I was going, even though I hadn't been there in years and I couldn't name the place. I couldn't park at my dad's house either, so I found a spot in a small lot surrounded by woods. The county had designated the woods behind my dad's house as a park, and that was a change from when I was growing up.

Some things do change.

I picked up the high-tension line trail at a point more west than where I used to enter it. I no longer could walk from my dad's house directly to the trail. Twenty minutes later, I was at a familiar spot on the trail. I approached the grey rock. The temperature sweltered, and sweat poured off me, down my arms, from my brows to my hands, which pulled out my journal. I stood on the rock, turned toward the City, which was a barely distinguishable smudge of grey in smog, the Twin Towers no longer standing. At the top of my lungs, I read out loud to it:

> I'm fucking sick and tired of living like this. When I am thirty, I will have it together in every necessary way. When I think about the future and how much closer I am to death just by living another day, I remember life should be seized. But I can't. I hate me I hate everything I hate this I hate my body I hate my mind I am out of control I am out of control I am out of control I can't handle anyone or anything and I don't understand I don't understand I can't sit still I can't stop crying I am out of control I hate everything I hate everything and I just want to die.

35: Kingston, NY

I went into the cold and quiet house, upstairs to my room and office. I smiled at the sight of a pickle-jar vase full of freshly cut marigold buds on my desk. Mom's touch. Another freelance gig had ended. I was mentally exhausted from fighting with the City: fighting with myself.

At least there was this, my own office, my droppings: A pile of papers on the desk, laid out and labeled with Post-it Notes: Tuesday. Thursday. Friday, next to the pickle jar of marigolds. I threw my backpack to the side and looked at my watch. 3.30pm. The quiet and stillness were suddenly broken—My mom. Her smooth and caw-like voice. Shouting something up the stairs.

"What?"

Her reply is muffled. I shouted down again: "What?"

"You want coffee?"

"Oh. Sure," I said. I waited a moment.

I heard a shuffling up the stairs. She burst through the door to my office with a steaming mug and shoved it right onto my desk.

"Come!" she said in a rush. "I have to show you something!" She ran back out.

I bit my tongue. I didn't want to get up—I had just gotten home. But I followed her anyway, leaving the mug behind. How long has she been waiting to pounce like this?

I find her on the front porch. "The squirrels were having Thanksgiving in October. They always munch on the pumpkin. Rats," my mom said softly, looking down.

I turned my gaze to follow hers, saw a mess of pumpkin bits trailing from the concrete porch to the end of the driveway.

"Oh well," she said. She took a plastic bag out of her pocket, shook it out, laid it down, motioned for me to take the two corners at my feet. She gently scootched the pumpkin onto the makeshift gurney. We lifted it and walked carefully to the backyard. The late afternoon October pale sun stood pall bearer to the tossing of the pumpkin guts.

Mom and I let the gurney down, then she picked up large pumpkin pieces, threw them hard against the ground. They smashed into smaller bits. She laughed harder. I'm afraid she'll lose her breath. "I need a cigarette," she said. Quickly, she turned around, flew up the short back-porch stairs, and into the house. Gone. Swallowed up. Disappeared from the outside world.

I remained with the pumpkin bits, next to my artificially-bright orange converse, desperately tattered and old. I looked at my neon orange Casio watch—I'd been home for all of five minutes. The pumpkin bits, the shoes, the watch: desperately tattered portrait, an apt visualization for how I felt in my life.

Slowly, I followed my mom inside, quietly, walking upstairs to my office. I saw her out of the corner of my eye, in the room across the hall from the office, having her cigarette inside the house. The window was open. Blank look on her face. Smooth machine motion—burning stick to mouth, inhale, chest puff, burning stick from mouth, mouth to window, smoke blown out the screen...

"Mom," I said—

"Not now!" she snapped.

Oh, right. Her cigarette time was her time. I was not supposed to disturb her when she smoked. This was mom. She was confusing like that. This was home. I felt safe.

In my office: a hand-painted bench that my younger brother and I painted; our initials on it; our paint splotches in random drops. The cardboard carpet piece half the size of the room, with random thoughts, and scribbles, and doodles. The scrap of red carpet on the other side, with lines of white and yellow... the floor length purple curtains that now, in the weak morning light, are casting a soft purple glow. A pink glittery hula hoop suspended from the ceiling with white ribbon and pink shower curtain hooks. The 3-foot-tall fake sunflower that was given to me by my older brother when I was 18, an item that has travelled the world and back—currently tied to black metal shelves with sparkly pipe cleaners: green, silver, blue. The "Leipzig—Brig" train sign that I lifted on a trip to Germany in 1997, when I rode trains across Europe. It sits on the jamb above the door. The oversized Oktoberfest mug, -that's from the trip in 1997 to Germany. The mug is propped against the outer door to the office, holding it shut because the door isn't level. The bulletin board—an upcycled garment rack with cardboard attached by shower curtain hooks—those things are useful. One side was covered with flyers, and notes, and pics, and to-do post-its (purple); the other side was covered with 6 other colors of post-its, color-coordinated with to-do items that related to the different projects I had going on. The two small metal pipes on the bottom hold two small cardboard box tops—overturned, full of project bags and books. The armless black office chair. I detached and threw out the arms a long time ago. A flatscreen, two laptops, a DVD player, an external hard drive, a stereo receiver, a three-hole punch, and a paper guillotine. The prized possession I call the "monster bike," my mechanical bike that I rode for hours at a stretch when my mind started to race and I had nowhere to go in this small town; the monster bike sat in the corner, facing the window, covered in collage with monster stickers, concert tickets taped on, and pictures of pumpkins that I also taped to the surface. Two panels of brown, jungle-print fabric hung on the walls; one behind the flatscreen, and one on the closet door. A UFO poster with a caption that read "I want to believe," a picture of Tully from Ghostbusters, the scene where Egon has him strapped with wiry thingies and a spaghetti-colander-like contraption on his head to test his brain waves. A Dunkin' Donuts cup on the makeshift desk—a piece of plywood laid across two trestles—contains markers; a toilet paper tube, fixed to a square cardboard coaster with blue tape—holding pencils. Three small white baskets hold computer cords. Four piles of neatly ordered papers—work to be done, labeled by dates and times. A pica ruler laid on top of my lap desk that laid on top of the floor pillow.

This work space wasn't transient.

This was home, and even though I was in my early thirties, and I didn't want my life to look like this, it did.

I swung my hips, from right to left, and adjusted my knees. I looked out the window in the closet. I went to my cherry red laptop, perched on my slab-of-wood-over-sawhorses desk. I pressed the on button. I was going to work: I was going to write.

Mom had always supported my desire to write a book. What I would do with my words, get them published, or let anyone read them--that was a different story.

Noon, the next day.

I got up, slipped on my orange Converse, and threw a vest and scarf over my shoulders. I peered out of my room before I exited—and I heard a snuffled snoring coming from my mom's room. Middle of the day and she was sound asleep.

I went downstairs, out the door, and walked past the stone buildings to the corner. It was a short walk down the street to the Chinese place. The small town around me yielded passersby as moving bits of energy. Women with tattoos and undone hair. Tourists. A Catskill flavor of micro-tiny-something professionals—the beards on the boys and boots on the ladies give it away —and the men and women native to the historically Dutch town had soft white skin and soft white eyes. A bunch of gardens and old buildings, too.

I looked up to my right and saw the tall brick façade of the backside of an old vaudeville theater. "Wall Street" said some painted-on advertisements.

See? This place even has City street names. That damned place haunts me everywhere I go.

There was a small park on the corner, where the street my mom's house was on bisected another street. I looked at the tufts of tall grass, the leaves on the still-green lawn.

My stomach grumbled again. I looked across the street: Chinese: the token Chinese food place, run by a small family, all three generations of them, in any town. It wasn't great but it wasn't bad; their sesame noodles could be spiced up with siracha—yes, I thought, noodles with sesame sauce and siracha. That's it.

I entered the small restaurant. The plastic placard above the counter grabbed my attention for a moment, long enough to realize this is probably the same plastic placard that other Chinese food places displayed, the one that shows plates that never look like the actual food you receive. "Hi," I said. "Cold sesame noodles, please. And a vegetable soup."

"Size?" said the woman, but it sounded more like an un-ending "sigh?"

"Large," I answered. I started to say that I really liked the sesame noodles, my effort at making conversation, but it didn't go very far. The woman replied "Oh yes, yes, noodles good."

I heard her call out my order in Chinese. One of the cooks shouted back. I sat on a ripped vinyl seat. The row of chairs was right in the line of the door, and a cool breeze slipped through.

"Here you go," said the woman, emerging back at the counter with a small brown paper bag. I got up quickly, paid, took my food, and left.

My feet moved fast. I peeked at the small park on the corner: electric. Now, the tufts of grass and leaves looked turned on, looked like suddenly they would lurch, forward, grabbing me—*Stop stop stop.*

I held my bag of noodles and soup into my chest, held it firm, as I barreled home, head looking at the ground.

I got back to the house and flew up the stairs.

I relaxed when I made it to my office. I heard the soft cadence of the snore through the heating vent. I placed the bag on my desk, and walked over to the windows. I used one finger to part the curtain, peered out, watched a few people walk down the sidewalk of my street. The parking lot and county courthouse, across from my house, buzzed with activity. People walking around, carrying files, cell phones.

I let the curtain fall back, closed, and returned to my desk. As I ate, I decided I would shut off my laptop. There was only so far that I could venture today. I folded the last strings of sesame noodles around my chopsticks. I took the bottle of siracha—a fixture on my desk—and doused the tahini-covered strings with hot sauce, gulped the mouthfuls down. I felt a few bubbles in my stomach. My tongue burned, but I liked it. I finished my meal, put the soup in the upstairs kitchenette fridge, and crossed back to my own space.

Twelve hours later, it was the middle of the night, and I was laying with my head on my desk. I was startled by a knock on my bedroom door.

"Yeah?" I softly called out.

"I love you," my mom's voice said.

"Love you, too," I replied. I curled my toes and pressed my feet harder into the unfinished wooden floor. I heard a flutter of papers as my head knocked some notebooks off the desk. Streetlight peeked into the space between where my curtain hung strangely, and I saw the peeling paint on the ceiling. There was a hole that was sort of patched—my mom insisted on leaving it as it was—and it looked like the lathe around the hole was starting to crack more. The light from the window seemed to highlight this, too.

38: New York City

After living in the Hudson Valley for a while, I felt grounded. I started to think that I could handle a day in the City, a free day, to wander the streets and follow the stimulation; one day, there and back, I told myself. This wasn't a day to work, this was a day for my own work. My writing.

I walked to the bus station from my mom's house, rode the bus directly to Port Authority in midtown, hopped a train to the village, and got out on Eighth Street. I walked on until I sat on a bench in Washington Square Park.

I unfolded a piece of paper from my neon, zebra-striped Pan Am bag. On it, my running creative-writing-brainstorm of the week. The words were a mystery to me, as if I had written them in a fugue. There they were, staring up from the paper:

How to Use the Memory Device

Start the circuit at the first block. Let go of the assumption you are in control. Connect to

the next circuit by turning at the next block. The programming is
in control. Continue;

turn; continue, so forth. The programming is your memory. For
optimal memory-inducing experience, try the tunnels and the
bridges. The structures have direct access to

the source of all Fire. Your Memory knows you.

I didn't know what it was supposed to mean, or do, or be. I didn't
know when I had written it, sometime that week. Herein was the
story of my life. Gaps in memory, memories that felt present, haunted
by imagery that had sentience. Each time I looked at the words
on the paper, they turned into pixels that assembled into information
and burned through ink onto fibers of wood-turned paper.

I stuffed the writing back in my bag.

But the train of thought:

Haze over my mind.

I had imagined that I would write pamphlets like this for all cities I
had loved and used to hide in. "Smart user design" and "intelligent
live-work spaces" were buzz phrases. That seemed so impersonal.
The concrete jungles were my friends. The cities spoke to me, and
here, in the greatest City on Earth, I disappeared. Sensation overcame me when I turned on music, and fell into myself, separate,
observing, the messiness of millions of humans milling in contained
areas, the smells, and sounds, the crimes, the foods, the traffic and the
stores upon stores, tunnels that were full of things that would taunt
me if I entered; public space full of unseen monsters who moved
along cracked roads, broken roads that were slow travel routes by
foot and even slower by vehicle. Haziness lifting.

Where am I?

I was walking down Eighth Street when I caught a glimpse of myself in a storefront. I gasped. I looked frumpy—bundled against the winter cold in a scarf, and long jacket, and saddled with bags; I never went anywhere without too many notebooks. They, too, were part of my armor. I looked again at a different window, saw a mannequin, and thought it came to life. I saw Fire in her eyes. She wasn't a faux-human, no longer just a display; she was a coil of hot anger that rose up in me and came to life through the City.

Illusion, full force.

I was controlled by the City Memory device. I moved through the cool, wet City, taking me further into myself, I became thoughts only lived, didn't breathe. The sidewalk changed, again became a barreling river of water. (I imagined) water flowed by my foot, then stalled at my ankles, then licked the bottom of my pants. I looked up, around. The City looked back at me—dull gunmetal grey of towering buildings; dull shine off square windows of glass and plastic; dull reflections of dull mirror images, hundred-fold, kaleidoscopic, broken, tangles of more square windows.

Some fucking Memory device, I thought as I remembered the creative writing in my bag. My memory is alive.

The mannequin followed me, gazed down her long nose, her face in the half-light becoming more severe than usual. She tapped her brow with her forefinger. It was my mind but it only wanted her touch. I wondered when the signal—a receiver for the signal, rather—was attached. Could I break away from her?

I bowed my head in shame. I thought of a sock, a broken pencil, and pennies lying on the floor behind the passenger seat of some taxi. Like the memories I held, they had been there for years, discarded.

I heard the mannequin in my head. She was the avatar of a wild woman inside me: "You always fail me. Can't you see? The City is yours if you want it. Become it, like me, set me free. Stop cowering. Damn humans. You know they are testing you, yet you resist me. You are with me, and I am infinitely wiser than you. Chaos is the path to enlightenment."

A burning piece of emotion pierced the back of my throat, and I tasted blood. Then the mannequin's voice stopped. I chewed on the sour saliva and then swallowed.

What the fuck?

She was right—I was too scared to give in, too scared to confront the ghosts of memory that haunted me, and I knew I couldn't go on like this. I started to shake. I felt myself losing control.

The streets, the stratums of asphalt, thick with pedestrians and pedestrian-motored cars.

The mind: Took from me as it pleased.

Sirens pierced through the smoke.

I heard them through the thick sinuous ear-windows.

A hundred buildings burning along what were my streets. The Memory Device's signal took them. It took people. It had me. And it will kill me now.

My skin crawled with anticipation. I knew I could harm I myself. I wanted it.

Did I? Fuck.

The mannequin walked behind me, smiling, teeth glowing orange.

She matched the sky.

I looked down at my hand, which clutched the paper.

What the fuck? I picked it up, held it before my face, then dropped it onto the ground, into a rivulet of streaming, dirty liquid that floated around me. I watched the paper dissolve into the water (Or was it fire?). A numb sensation suddenly surrounded me. I didn't know where I was, if I had been consumed, and I had floated out of my body—Did it matter?

I turned away, caught a glimpse of the mannequin, who still followed me, whose smile was growing in intensity. Colors moved over her face. They flashed from orange into rainbows of terror, and I knew it wasn't her terror. She was feeding on the ruptured waves of emotion. And she was coming for mine. My fear. My confusion. "The City With Memory Device," I said out loud.

She looked at me coyly.

----waves of water rolled by me, licked at my legs----

The City went dark. Debris lay piled on the sidewalk as I walked. I was sickened every time I cast a glance back. My fractured vision cooed for her touch. She reached out to me, a demon in heat, part of the City machine.

The mannequin started to hum a tune, something I couldn't swallow—

I cringed at her sour notes that floated triumph to me. She was going to win; I was succumbing to the madness.

Sounds from the street interrupted my train of thought.

A vehicle skidded to a halt in the embers, and a door opened suddenly.

"Hey," somebody called out. "Are you okay?"

I looked down, realized I had fallen to my knees. My bag had spilled on the concrete. I was crying. I looked at the woman behind the wheel. "Fuck off!" I yelled. She pulled the door toward her, slammed it, and stared through the window.

The mannequin had disappeared.

I felt for my skin, my legs, my arms, because I couldn't tell my body from the City now. Sweat stung my eyes, hot against the cold wind. A smell of gasoline floated by. I gathered my belongings, got up, and ran for the nearest subway entrance—there, I would catch a train up to Port Authority and get on a bus out of there. I had almost blown a fuse. The City almost got me. I tried to look inside myself in the mirror that was New York City. I couldn't handle it. I had to go home and hide.

31: Kingston, New York

The thruway 87 was a straight shot—one direct line, up and down. Miles between exits. The mountains and fields that flanked the sides seemed to stand firm behind glass, just like pieces on display. Back to the Hudson Valley. Back to my mom's house, who would probably be sitting by the window, smoking when I arrived.

I was caught in reverie between the rolling apple orchards, the Catskills on the left, the endless parade of trees to the right, the immobility of the vista, the grace through which I moved through it and although I was in motion, the view out the window stayed the same. The trees bore bright red, orange, and yellow leaves. The colors were strong. The grey sky highlighted the vibrancy.

I turned my gaze from the window. The man sitting next to me was dirty. A white powder lay like dust on his denim jacket. Dandruff, or dust, I thought. His hair was ruffled. He clutched a duffel bag tightly to his lap. If I had to guess from his smell, Doritos were his continual dinner. His breath that came out in labored meter stank like Cool Ranch.

He shifted the bag in his lap. We caught glimpses of one another—swiftly our heads turned away. I went back to looking out the window, but his essence lingered. I nonchalantly looked down at our hips to make sure they weren't touching. I didn't even move my head, just the eyes. My ass was on my side of the seat, and his separate. It was the one thing I hated about this bus line—there weren't true bucket seats, and the only divider we had was the armrest, which didn't keep me completely severed from whomever sat next to me.

I was sure I didn't know him, but I couldn't shake an odd sensation of being connected to him somehow. A partner in mind paranoia.

I looked in my bag that was wedged between my feet on the floor, and drew out the pencil and clipboard. It wasn't well-lit in the bus cabin, not enough light to write, so I pressed the button for the light above the seat. A blob of piss yellow fell onto my lap.

I stole one more look at him without moving my head, then I positioned the clipboard on my leg, put the pencil tip to the paper, and waited… settling into a hazy, dusty cloud in my mind.

I didn't have my headphones in because my player was dead. I didn't want to plug it in because that meant I would be entering the Filthy Man's space. The bus was full and as quiet as a library—so quiet that I heard the split-splat-split… drops of rain against the fiberglass windows as soon as they started to fall. A rumbling sound over the hum of the bus in motion. Thunder fast approaching. There was nowhere I could go, and I didn't want to make a sound.

I turned my head back toward the window, drifted…

The bus rolled into the small town in a slow, lapping way. The subtle rum-a-chug-chug from the motor and the wheels came to a lazy stop under the sagging portico. We bus riders got up in a dull fash- ion, slowly, stiffly, stretched our arms and legs in a weird manner that I imagined to be like robots stretching—there was not much room between the overhead compartment and the seats—stick- ing appendages out into whatever space we could find in the cramped quarters.

This felt like a time warp; time sticky trap; time slow motion. The recycled air of the bus cabin—perhaps that dulled the senses and slowed the body down, and that's why the exit was belabored. I saw bright leaves outside swirling around in gusts of invisible wind, re-landing on the grayed-out pavement of the parking lot.

I finally folded into the aisle.

As I neared the door, a breeze—a cold breeze--from outside the bus blew in. I was suddenly more awake. I zipped my sweatshirt, threw my backpack over my right shoulder, dug my hands into my pockets, bounced down the stairs, through the door, and started to walk up the street to my mom's house.

33: Kingston, New York

"So what brings you here today?"

"I'm—" I couldn't get any words out. Snot ran down my face, and I was shaking so hard I thought the tears would fly off and into the air around me. "I was, my mind is out of control—"

"What makes you say that?" she asked, her voice a balm, warm, thick and soothing. The therapist, whose face of warm cheeks and soft hair, gazed kindly at me.

My chest heaved. More snots started to slide out of my nose as I continued on. "I can't stop I can't stop I can't stop," I said, the words rolling fast off my tongue. "My mind explodes and my body—it's… I …" And then I say it. "It's hard to live."

It was the first time I met with this therapist. She asked me to describe myself. I started with the basics: I am a white girl of Polish American heritage from northwestern New Jersey—I grew up in the woods. I'm from a blue-collar family, the kind that clings tightly to red county lines and pick-up trucks and little league football games. As a kid, I felt like I was different. I was often home alone.

My dad called the house repeatedly throughout the day, but never said, "Hello" when I picked up. He always asked, "What are you doing?"

"I'm sitting around, thinking."

"Get up and do something. Go feed the chickens. Go mow the lawn. Go help your brothers work in the garage. Go clean out the—"

I usually hung up mid-sentence.

"That was a long time ago, I know," I said, shaking my head. "He used to say that I couldn't be a writer. He used to tell me that if I didn't get a job, I'd end up like my mother."

"What's wrong with that?" the therapist asked.

I shook my head. Instead, I told her I got really angry when I had to stay at his house as a little kid, so I used to pack food in a backpack, put a few books in, too, and walk the old mine trails in the woods. I walked for hours. My favorite trail was the one that wound up a hill dotted with high-tension power lines. The area around it was always kept a little clearer than the woods. It was a nice spot. And there was a small boulder on top of the hill, and when I sat on it, I had a view due east, of the Twin Towers. Fifty miles from there to New York City. For as long as I could remember, I longed for those concrete strongholds.

"What did your mom say about your desire to hide in the City?"

"She—" I paused, "she just left me alone. My parents were divorced, but they talked nearly every day. Well they didn't *talk* talk. Besides, I hated being at my dad's house. In the middle of the night, the phone would ring—his construction shop's lines were forwarded to his house—getting him out of bed to do something for somebody. There was always something he needed to build, fix, excavate and in the winter, plow. Eat, drink, work, repeat. But if I was at my mom's, no one called."

"What else?"

"She had a job, sometimes. A retail factory. An office at a construction business. But she also spent a lot of time at home. Crying. When she went to the hospital, she just—" I paused.

"Why did she go to the hospital?"

I paused again, considering all the labels that my mom has had: clinically depressed. Major depression. Affective disorder. I thought of the times I had to drive her to a social worker's office. I thought of her house that was always a mess. The weeks on end my mom didn't get out of bed. The weeks when she was an inpatient at a psychiatric facility.

"And your family didn't help her? What did your dad do?"

I bit my lip. "Most of the time, they didn't know. I don't know, maybe my brothers did, but they were usually at my dad's house. It was always, *oh, your fucking mother.* Your mother just being your mother. And we never talked about it. Full stop."

"You never talked about her mental illness?"

"No."

"Not even with your mom?"

"No. You just don't bring it up, and then it doesn't exist."

The therapist shifted in her seat. "So when did you come to the Hudson Valley?"

"Two years ago."

"Why did you come here?"

"I like the town because it was gritty and green with tree-lined streets and views of the Catskills to the west. Some run-down houses. Empty storefronts. And I could get a bus to New York City right down the street." I paused, then added, "My mom bought a house here two and a half years ago. I could stay with her."

I sat on the therapist's couch in her neutral, peaceful, crystal-filled office, and I felt like I was starting to unfold, or, that the room was unfolding around me. A nakedness that felt like a moth buffering my ears with soft wings; more questions:

"And how long have these hallucinatory episodes been happening?" she asked.

"For a while. All my life, actually."

24: Newton, New Jersey

Mom and I were on a QuickChek ride. She had just been released from the hospital. I was looking for something for us to do that involved minimal interaction with the outside world. I drove, mom sat, on the hunt for cheap coffee and bagels. We were pulling through a different small town, one with a center green where the traffic slows for pedestrians. The car rolled slowly before a red light. I looked over to the passenger side window and noticed a small kitschy-looking shop. I thought about going in. But I couldn't muster the strength.

"Let's go," my mom suddenly said.

I turned my head—the sound of her voice was something that jarred me from time to time.

The light changed, so I turned my blinker on, then pulled into a side-street parking spot.

I got out, then walked around the car and opened her door. I gently took her hand and guided her out—or I tried to. Mom pulled her hand quickly back. She stood up, flat eyes, face down, and started to cross the sidewalk.

I let her.

We approached the store front and looked in the window—there were trays of silver jewelry, silver charms, and bracelets, and more; this is what had caught my eye from the car. A perfect beam of light made the pieces glisten and sparkle.

We went in, falling into a shop full of colorful fabric, bags, wall hangings, incense, batik wood, and cheap silver jewelry.

Then, she spoke: "You need that one." Mom pointed to one charm that was a music ball, and it had gold pieces of continents on it—it was the world. "You need that one. You're gonna write a book and be somebody in the world."

"It's the last of those that we have," said the shopkeeper, a young woman with a lean face and loud skirt. "Twenty dollars," she said.

Mom reached into her pocket and put out her credit card. I didn't even know she had one with her. I shook my head. "No, Mom, I've got cash."

"No," she said. She never took her gaze off the ball—her dead-to-the-world gaze. "You need this and I am paying for it. Always listen to your heart."

I watched the transaction happen: The shopkeeper took the card. The shopkeeper ran the card. I was handed the little silver ball. I jingled it. It sounded like delicate metal chimes, as if the shake of the sound soothed something in me; a shake, a gift, from my mom to me.

The shopkeeper smiled at us.

Mom and I walked back out of the shop. I put my arm gently on her shoulder as I started to lead us out. Neither of us said goodbye. We had left the store, and after we got into the car, I fiddled with the latch on my silver chain, got it open, then slid the ball onto the chain that I was wearing. I closed my eyes; and clasped my new charm.

A sweet, warm feeling overcame my face. I said "I love it, mom!" then I turned my head—

She was staring out the window. Seated. Buckled. Lit cigarette in her hand, the ash tip an inch-and-a-half long and ready to drop on her lap.

I leaned over, cupped one hand under the cigarette, gently tapped it with my other hand, caught the ashes, and turned toward the window. I blew the ashes out.

I held my gaze out the window, then turned the key in the ignition. I pulled out onto the road and through the yellow traffic light.

33: Kingston, New York; Denville, New Jersey

I sat in my office, on the second floor of my mom's house, and I had a pile of notebooks by my side. These were ones I kept during my initial recovery in my early thirties. I spent a lot of time depressed and angry that I overlooked the obvious. I opened one notebook and took a green ballpoint pen and chose a letter "t" and circled it, then found a letter that was appealing (an "A") and circled that too, completing the piece with a line connecting the two—a geometry of fractured mental space appears. It's a map of my mind, a topography, and I am inside those words, and I have bipolar disorder.

Tears start to slide down my eyes.

I pushed the notebooks aside.

I had bought a box of Entenmann's devil's food cake with chocolate icing on the way home from the therapist. Food is medicine she said. Try writing out your thoughts instead of going into them. And I could start by taking a fresh look at things I've done. Ways I've acted. A new perspective on my life when I used the magic words "trauma" and "mental illness"; they filled in the blanks between me and the people around me and how we interacted (and didn't).

And so, I took a bite of cake and began again,

a slide into memory—

a fresh page in a notebook from my late thirties, the one where I acknowledge how trauma and mental illness have interwoven throughout my life and my parents are the literal examples of that: The mental reel starts with the taste association: Dad always had sweets on the counter. I eyed the Entenmann's cake box, hungry, while I listened to him droll on about me not having a real job, that I can't be a writer, that I should be working. I had gone to his house for a visit on a weekend trip out of the City. I expected to be berated; that's how my family talked to each other. And when you tell some-one something so many times, sometimes they start to believe it.

((blah blah blah))

"You know, Frankenstein," I said, cutting him off, "writing is great because it lets all the stuff you have inside, out. You keep too much inside. All you do is work work work."

He glared at me and I noticed his right eye was bloodshot. He looked clammy. "Frank, you look like shit, too. What's wrong with you?" I felt my stomach turn from the biting retort to serious concern. He really did look unwell.

"Nothing is wrong with me," he said, tossing back the rest of his tumbler of vodka.

Two weeks later, on a Tuesday morning, I was living in Greenpoint, Brooklyn, conjecturing what I was going to do with my life, hiding in the City, place of a million different faces, real and fake, drinking a morning tea.

The phone rang.

"Dad's in the hospital," my younger brother said. "You need to get here."

I had a hard time leaving the apartment: I remember feeling heavy, and head-cloudy, and I really didn't want to do anything especially not go home, to the foreign world across the river. I could only trust my feet. I walked to the subway, waited fifteen minutes for the G train, to the L, waited another twenty minutes. I cursed Greenpoint, Brooklyn, for its slow-moving transportation.

The next part of the memory: My ears became hot.

He laid in the ICU, in a hospital bed. A feeding tube had been taped to his cheek and led into his mouth. His body was covered in a sheet, and underneath that, a paper gown.

"I'm sorry about your dad," someone said. I shook my head in response but I didn't turn around to look who said that.

What do I do?

I approached the bed, took my dad's hand, which felt heavy, cold, clay-like; so I let it drop immediately.

I stood up, over him.

I felt puke in my mouth.

My insides were ready to come out.

I left. Out of the room, into the hallway, down the direction where no one saw me. A janitor was standing in front of the elevator, whistling, waiting for the elevator to arrive. His cart was full of plastic gloves, plastic bags, and disinfectant.

I left the stairwell and walked around the main corridor of the hospital, trying door after door, until I found one that opened, a vacant bathroom. I locked myself in. I laid down on the floor. I stayed there.

33: Kingston, New York; South Orange, New Jersey

I sat in my office, on the second floor of my mom's house, and I had a pile of notebooks by my side. These were ones I kept during my manic years in my early twenties. I went unchecked. Unaccountable. Until *that day* happened and then the stuff in the notebooks changed. Late twenties: notebooks full of utter desperation and an unwillingness to live.

Tears start to slide down my cheeks.

I pushed the notebooks aside. I couldn't leave the house. I had that much control over myself—or, I had no control over my body. It wouldn't move.

My therapist had given me a choice. I could go to a hospital for inpatient treatment—the hallucinations, the chattering teeth, the tears, a mixed state. Or I could do the work as outpatient, supported by a constellation of healthcare professionals. I was in a limbo—between the mania and the depression. My mind unable to make meaningful meaning. My body that would have exploded off of me, had it the choice. Maybe my mind would have exploded, too, if I wasn't invested in this *work*. I believe every moment is a moment that I reach for a lightness in my being—inner peace—and that meant I had to move through frozen time, the place my mind refuses to move from.

I opened a notebook and took a pink ballpoint pen and chose a letter "q" and circled it, then found a letter that was appealing (an "e") and circled that too, completing the piece with a line connecting the two—a geometry of fractured mental space appears. It's a map of my mind, a topography, and I am inside those words, somehow.

I had bought a box of Entenmann's devil's food cake with chocolate icing, on my way home from the therapist's that day. Food is medicine the therapist had said. She also said, "try writing out your thoughts instead of going into them."

I dove for the cake.

a slide into memory—

The first bite tasted like chemicals—I ate it fast, the whole thing—the cake bites, the memory flashes, the morsels of flour and sugar and preservatives breaking down in my body, the seizing in my throat, the fight hard to stay with it, the tightening in my throat and the tears that wanted to ooze out of my eyes.

Write it out. See it. Transform it.

It is a rapid mental cycle: a fresh page in the notebook: taste association: and I was out of this space and time.

I made my way down the hallways, half floating, half wandering. I found the large metal doors to the wing of the doors that lock-behind-you. A psych ward. I buzzed to be let in.

This place feels dead, even in memory.

I looked behind me and watched the heavy metal doors float shut—a soft, air-filled swing then final CLANK as they caught and the lock engaged. A light on the security camera—perched at the top right corner of the doorframe—blinked.

I took one careful step after the other. One heavy foot after the other. One rubber-soled sneaker (the "squeep!" sound in the memory echoed) after the other on the floor (squeep!). The hallway opened up to the nurses' bay: a spaceship-like command berth, where the captain, aka head nurse, stood over the fleet of other nurses who watched a monitor. A persistent staccato beep-beep-beep coming from somewhere.

"Excuse me," I said. "I'm here to see my mom."

Captain nurse looked up. She had crumbs on her lips. The three other nurses turned their heads. All of them had cake crumbles on their faces. A half-empty box of Entenmann's devil's food cake lay on the counter.

I heard one of the nurses ask: "Should we call security?" Anyone who exhibits strange behavior in the ward is suspect. The nurses are trained to corral such people.

I turned. "No need to call security. I'll behave."

I felt my eyes crossing, my mind blurring—for a second, I realized that all the patients in here were invisible, in office-like-rooms with solid walls, hidden away behind ward doors and I shuddered violently.

"Your mother will recover in two weeks. Not a problem," the head nurse said impersonally, detached, with an impersonal smile. She stood behind me.

The woman who looks like me—her hair frizzed out, her face pale and expressionless, body wearing a bland hospital-issued covering gown—didn't move. She lay in bed. Her eyes looked like wet marbles in sockets. They contained the vacancy of B-movie monster puppets. I couldn't look at her, so I immediately turned back. "She doesn't recognize me," I said to the head nurse, but she had already gone back to her station.

33: Kingston, New York; Rockaway, New Jersey

When I was twenty-four, my dad, who was forty-nine at the time, dropped dead of a ruptured brain aneurysm. On the very same day, I learned my mom was receiving ECT shock therapy at a hospital a half hour away. My mom has been disabled ever since.

I brought myself to write about the funeral after another box of Entenmann's cake. The scene came out as flat and sharp as I had experienced it: My mom, escorted by her sister, walked forward like she was an elderly woman needing help to cross the street; my mom stopped right in front of my dad's casket.

a slide into memory—

I swooped up and in to stand by my mom's side. I scanned her face to see if there was any register of emotion. None: face heavy and plain as unmolded clay. Her eyes were dull bulbs, still. I watched her stand over the body, look with those vacant eyes, touch with one outstretched finger the made-up face of my dad, and then turn, with vacant eyes, to look at me and say: "I'm ready to go now."

"Do you want me to take her home?" my aunt asked me.

"Sure," I replied, watching that word as it slipped out of my mind, a hazy, faint, pantomimed sound.

I looked at my watch: 1 minute. Mourning time: less than a minute.

My mom and my aunt, one vacant and one somber, wobbled out of the funeral home, my aunt's round frame once again guiding my mom, whose frizzed out hair and potato-sack hospital attire moved without any real animation.

Through a stream of light from the door as it opened… they walked out.

But then—

my paternal grandmother walked in with her husband. Then a few other Polish relatives. The door shut behind them. Light cut out. The room filled with a soft scent of onion and apples.

They went straight to the casket, gathered and stared at my dad's dead body. The emotions flowed out in their wails.

I didn't know what to do, so I stepped cautiously back to the jungle of floral arrangements. I went in a corner where I was out of their eyesight, watched them, saw their sad eyes moving in sad faces. They all kept a gaze on him, my dad, in the casket; some of the women clutched rosaries. I felt a tightening in my chest, and I realized I wasn't breathing. I let out a sigh, then checked my watch. 3:25pm.

3:46: My paternal grandmother and her entourage finally get up and hurry out of an entrance on the opposite side of the funeral parlor as my paternal grandfather entered. A light-beam-filled door way—

(They don't talk to one another.)

3:53: my dad's brother, his kids walked in; my dad's sister, too. More of the immediate family.

The sound of soft crush-crush-crush of footsteps on the carpet. Soft mumbling. Dull light through the frosted windows. My grandfather lingers, rest of the family does, too.

4:02—and the room started to fill with more people. More and more people. Some of the Latino workers my dad had hired. A few of my older brother's friends. The first two rows of the seating area were full. I looked around the non-descript house—funeral parlor, the pale blue and dull white insides, the profuse number of flowers and thick air of mall perfume, the many living bodies gathered. These were the same bodies who didn't tell my dad to slow down and who didn't understand my mom's mental illness. These bodies didn't *talk* talk. My head hurt, so I started to trace the stripes on my capri pants, up and down, up and down. I waited for the opportunity to get lost in the City again.

38: New York City

I was in a tunnel, walking from Grand Central Station, to that week's gig. I'll have an inbox full of instructions and a pile of jobs on my temporary desk, which is right in the middle of the editorial department. I'll be alone on the night shift. My desk will be covered in flowers: sweet-smelling, delicate white and peach carnations from the deli down the block. I bought them a few days ago. It was part of my gratitude practice. I liked having flowers where I worked, literally and metaphorically. I'm grateful I'm me, carrying my neon, zebra-striped Pan Am bag, wearing a long green trench coat. The mp3 player was playing electronica. These were things that were constants over the years.

I turned the corner, and the passage was clear. I've got two-hun-dred-thirty-two steps to the door that will take me to the staircase that will take me to the lobby, past a Starbucks, to a security guard who will ask for my badge—as in, confirming that I have permission to be in this organ of the City—and then he will approve my badge and allow me up the escalators, which will bring me to the elevator, which will take me up to the seventeenth floor, which is where I'm working tonight.

There's a janitor whose name I always forget—he'll be there. But he was awkward and always too eager to talk to me. That's how I know he doesn't live in the City, that he takes a train from a town an hour and a half away to work.

"You ride the train to sweep floors?"

"Yep." His acne, metal-band t-shirt, and wiry unruly hair tell me that he doesn't care much about appearances, and by extension, norms. He says he finds comfort in sweeping the floors and emptying the trash of an office in the City as it sleeps.

"Wow," I said. The City works on all of us in its own way. I listened to the squeaks of the rolling garbage can for ten minutes, sound diminishing—telling me that he's left my side and was now clear across the floor.

It's 2am when I finished editing. I'm staying in the City tonight at a friend's, so I'm going to the subway and not Port Authority. I walked back down the hallway to the elevators, to the escalators, and past the security guard's post. He wasn't there. I'm the only one in the building—except for the janitor, upstairs. It is an intimate moment inside the building, myself. I went across the floor and lobby. Starbucks was closed. I walked through corridors to the subway whose tracks were built into tunnels that wound underneath the City, below the buildings that hold the material that reflects the chaos I have had inside.

Or, used to. I'm quiet now.

I stood on the edge of the platform, and I vomited, and I cried, and I wretched, and I screamed, and I let go. I'm standing by myself at the track in the subway station at Grand Central, and this didn't really happen, but it happened here on the page, and therefore it happened, and it has become part of my real life, and it healed me. It may not be factually true, but it is emotionally true. The experience of fiction and fact healed me.

39: Kingston, New York

The thruway was a straight, grey line. Billboard signs flanked the side and offered used cars, country fudge, and apple orchards. In sum, this and that.

I leaned back, propped on an elbow, my right foot over the dashboard fan. I looked down at my bare foot, steady on the gas pedal. I had purchased this van about a year ago. I used it to travel more, outside of the City and the Hudson Valley area. Public transportation couldn't take me where I wanted to go. The electronica transformed the roadway into a pathway through space. The volume was turned way up, and I couldn't feel anything around me and I flew fast, moving with the speed of sound.

I arrived at my mom's house, and turned off the electronica first, then the van. Dusk was setting in over the small town, and strident last beams of sunlight ricocheted off the glass window of the stone and wood houses, casting spotlights onto pieces of street art. The brick building directly across from the driveway lit up and the painted advertising—*Women's Clothing Store*—on its side caught my eye. I relished it. I had gazed upon it many times from the window of my office on the second floor. It was a constant. And this would be one of the last times I would see it. I had come to say goodbye to my mom and this place.

Coconut cake—fresh, local, made by the diner—was tonight's indulgent treat. I picked it up for us on my way to my mom's house. We ate with our fingers, shoveling the rich mouthfuls of sponge and icing, laden with sugar, which made my teeth hurt.

"Mom," I said. "I'm not coming to your funeral."

I admit, it came out of nowhere, but I felt compelled to say it, so I did. She didn't bat an eye. The frankness with which we addressed death was part of the unique bond that my mom and I shared.

"Okay. I don't remember your dad's funeral. So, it's fine if you don't come to mine. I don't want one, anyway."

My mom was in her late 60s and was permanently disabled due to motor skill damage from the ECT treatments. We prepared for her late life milestones that would affect both of us—death, disease, loss of her mind, freedom in my mind—by talking about them, like now, over food. My recovery demanded it of me, as much as my recovery demanded I take on the work of honoring the chaos of disorder and trauma. Mom never worked again after that hospital stay in which she received ECT. No—work is relative. My mom worked all the time—living is hard work.

I smiled. "And mom—thank you for believing in me. I finally finished my book. The one it took my whole life to write. I finally figured out what I wanted to say."

She looked up at me and smiled, a genuine smile, and said, "I'm so proud of you. You have achieved what I never could." She finished her cake, got up, patted me on the head, put her plate in the kitchen sink, and then turned. "I'm tired now. I'm going to take my afternoon nap."

"Okay."

She coughed lightly as she went down the hallway and made her way up the stairs.

And then suddenly, I was alone in a place that was once my sanctuary. Now I felt too separated from other people. Too hidden away. Too strong to hide behind chaos. And I needed to leave this place to continue to grow.

I got up, put my plate in the sink, and went up to my old office. A mirror hanging on the hallway wall caught my attention. I looked at myself. My brown shoulder-length hair sat loose on my shoulders, my nose and lip piercings hung with their rainbow titanium jewelry, asking you (asking me) to look at my face. The black crocus tattoo on my chest demanded attention, too. The delicate flower was set against a bursting mandala, exquisite fine lines and detail. Crocuses are the first flower to appear after winter, when the rawness of spring is sharp and the ground is opening upon itself for a new cycle of growth. The crocus symbolizes emergence. The crocus is a beacon. When the cycles of heaviness, darkness, and hibernation draw me underground, pull me away from community, and beckon me toward a time of quiet, I look at my crocus and remember I will reemerge. But I must bide the time in the places in my mind that feel cold, dark, and loveless. They too are part of my human experience.

A black line glyph is on my throat. It is the symbol of Chiron—the wounded healer archetype: it is Chiron who relates his story that the wound is also the medicine. The glyph reminds me to sit with my discomfort, and reflect. There is power in the shape of it for me—the power of memory and mastery over time. Time is a line. Time is rupture, realignment, and redrawing of shapes. Time is only mind.

The story of how I have been controlled by (unconsciously) or propelled by (consciously) the trauma and disorder I have in my mind, can be read in the symbolic language of my tattoos. I looked in the mirror and smiled. The silver world-ball charm hung just above my crocus. I shook it for good measure. The sound was balm to my ears; it contained the medicine of memory and future potential.

I woke up the next morning without the alarm, got up quickly. I heard heavy snores coming from my mom's room, so I wrote her a Post-it note—"See you soon, xo"—stuck it to the door and left.

I drove through the commercial part of town—a congested two-lane highway flanked by every single imaginable store. I pulled over at a Staples. Even though it wasn't even 9am, it was open. I made a couple copies of everything that I had written down and this manuscript. My hands shook as I did—I felt like there were a million eyes watching me. And I knew that from inside, there were. The same eyes that showed me inward, the space where the pictures turned movies played, and now the same eyes looked outward—surely, paranoid, someone, somewhere, somehow knew everything that I was doing. The eyes of the City. The eyes of chaos, controlled.

I left Staples and went to QuickChek, for coffee, then turned off onto a wooded county road that lead me deeper into the forest of the Catskills. I watch as patches of large and preposterous houses start to thin, how one mansion at the end of a long driveway sat with the lights out. I turned, continued on, slower, searched for a pull off--somewhere that I could burn.

I took a sip of my coffee. The air between the needle-laden fir trees was warm. Their shelter made the location discrete. I started the small fire with some bird's nest that had fallen out of a white birch tree. The hearth was on some freshly turned up earth, a circle I surrounded with some small stones I found nearby. Here is where I could complete my work. I turned the fire on with wooden matches and pith from a downed log. It caught easily. I burned the pages that I had copied that morning—the pages of the dreams from my journal, the pages of the conscious writing from a notebook, a draft of this manuscript. The burn was symbolic. The burn was catharsis. It doesn't matter that real life happens as it happens; I wrote my story of it and let go all of it, the good and the bad. I picked up some of the ashes and blew them away. I looked at them as they carried on the cold late morning wind and remarked how soft they were, like dust.

I rubbed some ashes between my fingers. They felt smooth, almost, like nothing. And then I laughed: "Nothing doesn't feel like nothing."

I put my hands on the earth around the belly of the burn, curled my fingers into cups, and I began to scoop. I dug into the warm dirt, and sprinkled it down, letting the embers of the fire smolder. I sprinkled dirt over my thighs, clothed in green cargo pants. I rubbed my right pointer finger across the top of my left forearm, traced dirt over the ink embedded in my skin: another tattoo: *Per ardua ad astra.* "Through work to the stars" it said, my own handwriting.

40: New York City

I'm sitting outside on a park bench in Central Park. I'm middle aged. Today, there was no one on the bench with me, there were no Canada geese running through the Great Meadow. There was no small, black deli plastic bag floating up over an American elm tree, no mom and baby, no teenage girl.

My notebooks were stashed in my purse to my side, and I don't feel particularly called to write in them. I wrote a book, this work you're reading, and I'm thinking about that. How it took me a long time. How I stopped and started. How writing is hard work. How creative expression heals.

The City was quiet because not many people are out, even though it's nearly 60 degrees. A rarity in this otherwise life-filled metropolis—but it's Christmas Eve. People are inside their homes, celebrating with family. Today, I am outside. I am free. I am calm. I am celebrating myself by basking in the empty space in the City. The ritual is symbolic.

I look at some scaffolding and realize the building it's on is going to be one hundred stories. And then I see that it's right next to another building where I went to work as a temporary employee, a gigger. I couldn't have held down a job back then, not with the chaos in my mind.

My work here is done. New York City doesn't reflect the world inside me anymore. There is nothing new to see here. It is on these pages.

Late 60s: A city in South America

The video phone beeps and displays an avatar, picture of me as a young girl with my strawberry blonde pigtails and a cherub face with squinty eyes and an upturned nose. I'm wearing a pink sweatshirt and maroon corduroy pants. I'm standing in front of a large bed of red and yellow tulips in front of a tree with white flowers. I'm holding a pink ball. I know that I was around three years old when the photo was taken.

The avatar reads the contents of the email in a high-pitched child-like voice: "Congratulations on your third best-selling fiction novel." The email is from my literary agent.

I was in my office, the one with a view over the sprawling city. I chose it to get out of the limelight of the publishing industry. There are great street markets and long, winding trails through the mountains that flank the urban center. In the dark, the mountains form a distinct shape—black. It is only when you look in the daylight you see them. Now was night, and the lights of the buildings look like stars within the cradle of the mountains.

I live in an apartment in a high rise, and sometimes I feel uncomfortable about being so far from the ground. So I've lined my walls with a hydroponic system. Blue roses and red geraniums and miniature palm trees flourish year-round, night and day. This is the garden in my office.

The entirety of my home is balanced in this design. Each room has its own: the kitchen, edible herbs like cilantro and parsley and rosemary, which I've never cared for but my adopted daughter loves. The large living room has sunflowers. The main bathroom, bamboo, and the bathroom in my master bedroom, jasmine.

I smiled and in a small mirror on my metal desk, I caught a glimpse of the wrinkles that form at the corners of my eyes. My long hair is streaked with silver. I'm wearing denim overalls with shoulder-brushing hoop earrings. The tattoos on my arms and chest have started to fade from a life of exposure to the sun. I wonder, as I often do, what my body would have looked like if I had my own children. Would stretch marks have added to the tattoos that are on my breasts and sternum? Would my thighs have earned girth? Would my ass have rounded out? Would my hair have more grey, and would I have decided to cut it short rather than keep it long?

Another message comes through—this time, a video recording from my adopted daughter: "Mom, I really want to go to Iceland. I'm obsessed with volcanoes. I like the idea that the Earth is alive. I want to see an eruption."

I smiled again… I didn't make her, but I see so much of me in her. She's a teenager having her own flights of fancy these days, which I can handle. She's come a long way from when she arrived to me. She was a writhing, screaming toddler. The adoption agency said she had been abandoned, and they believed that her parents were addicts. The agency said she would need a lot of patience and care. I said I've got that, plus an open heart and mind.

I sent my adopted daughter a video message back: "That sounds amazing! Tell me more over dinner?" I pressed send without replaying it to myself. I've gotten into the habit of re-listening to every sound I make. I'm getting comfortable with the smoothness in my mature voice. Sometimes, I schedule too many readings online in a day, and then I teach creative writing workshops to classes with hundreds of students. My voice is strong but my throat gets tired. I need to remember to rest my vocal cords more but that's hard to do when I am excited about teaching people how to write their own story. It's something that I could talk about all day; it's something that I have talked about my whole life. Exploring the potential of the creative process for transformation has been my life's work.

I stood up, stretched, and walked into the kitchen. Even though I'm a novelist, there aren't many printed books in my home. I converted most of my collection to digital archives. The volumes are easier to access that way. Some of my prized collection—a hand-bound volume of astrological writings from 1820, a first edition of SevenThirteen, my first book—are in pneumatic glass cases. The air ages pages like the sun ages skin. I walked down a short hallway whose walls are covered in framed pictures—my mom, my dad, my brothers, my friends, my teachers, my healers who met me in different places in my journey. Some are alive, and some are now dead; time has taken their life. But they are alive in me. When I look into their faces, I see books to be written, to be read, to read. There are pictures of New York City in the 1990s and 2000s, too. Those were my favorite times there. I love the inner chaos, now. The City was a mirror. It reflected me, even if I didn't want to see it. But surrender set me free from my prison. One of the pictures catches my eye, which it does every time I walk down the hallway. I'm wearing a dark green trench coat, and my beloved neon-zebra-striped Pan Am style bag dangles in one hand. A coffee is in the other. It's an iconic blue and white paper cup. The words "We are happy to serve you" are scrawled in a golden rod color in letters that are meant to look Greek. I still remember buying it from a coffee cart on the corner of Columbus Circle. I had been early to arrive at work that day, so I spent the extra time in Central Park. I remember my notebook pages fluttering in cool fall breezes. The black and white scarf I wore in the picture is pulled tight around my neck, framing my face in which I wear a Mona Lisa smile. My eyes, behind yellow frames, are squinted, too, but smiling. They speak to me now, still, as they spoke to anyone who was lost in their own darkness: I see you. I believe in you. You can work yourself out.

About the Author

Anastasia Wasko is an artist, writer, and energy worker from New York/New Jersey area and currently living in New Orleans, Louisiana. With a BA in Transpersonal Psychology from Sofia University (formerly Institute of Transpersonal Psychology), her creative output is largely informed by psychological processes and engaging with reality on the subtle, energetic level. Wasko's fiction and creative non-fiction writing have appeared in Space Cowboy's Simultaneous Times podcast, Thrive Global, and in *Journal of Exceptional Experiences*. Her debut work of autofiction *SevenThirteen* was self-published in 2003.

Read more at *anastasiawasko.com*.